Miracles Happen!

FLAVIA SUPPORTS THE LIFE-SAVERS FOUNDATION OF AMERICA

For More Information Or To Join The Flavia Club
Write To Flavia c/o Applause inc.

APPLAUSE INC.
6101 Variel Avenue
Woodland Hills, CA 91365-4183
© 1990 Flavia Weedn All Rights Reserved
Licensed By Applause Licensing
Printed in Italy
21764

Published And Distributed By Applause Inc.

ISBN 0-929632-11-7
Library Of Congress No. 90-81071

Designed By James O. Frazier

Flavia AND THE CHRISTMAS LEGACY

WRITTEN BY FLAVIA & LISA WEEDN

ILLUSTRATED BY FLAVIA WEEDN

Some called her Mama,
some called her
Gramma Syl,
but she was an angel,
and her magic
touched the earth
for awhile.

It is with love
that we dedicate
this book to her.

It was the day before Christmas Eve, and cold, as Flavia and her younger brother, Willie, walked down the street looking into store windows. It was a magical time of year because the sights and sounds of Christmas were everywhere. Flavia even thought she could taste Christmas in the air.

The family had drawn names for Christmas last Thanksgiving when they were all together, and now Flavia and Willie were trying to find just the right gifts for the names they had chosen.

Flavia knew it wouldn't be easy this year because there was very little money to spend and, since she had drawn Willie's name, she was trying very hard to keep him from knowing.

She knew this was all part of the excitement and magic that had always happened this time of year for as long as she could remember. The magic was because of Mama. Everyone knew it was Mama's most favorite time, and since Flavia and Willie believed Mama to be an angel, Christmas, no matter what, had always been very important and very wonderful at their house.

Flavia looked up at the calendar on the kitchen door, where she
and Willie had been marking the days, and saw that now there were only
two days left. She felt a tingling inside when she thought of Christmas…
and quietly wished that everyone in the world could share this wonderful
feeling.

It was almost dark now, and she looked at everything around her.
Mammo, her grandmother, was cutting out gingerbread cookies, while
Daddy tried to untangle the Christmas lights.

The room was still cold from when Daddy had opened the door and
brought in the Christmas tree. Flavia saw how small the tree was this
year…and knew it would have to be put on the table instead of the floor.
She wondered if Willie noticed.

Mama was baking bread dough stars for the tree and trying to make a cloth doll at the same time. Flavia's young uncle, Jack, had just hung the sleigh bells outside on the front door, and returned to the back room of the house where he would often go to write.

Jack was very special to her, and when she knew he was writing, she never bothered him…for she knew that words don't come easy sometimes.

Jack wrote poems and stories about how he felt inside…and how being alive was magic. He was very wise and a lot like a big brother to her. Jack knew about dreams and not giving up and about believing. He knew about all the wonderful things. He was a Dream Maker.

Flavia looked across the room at the someone new this Christmas...
for now there was a little baby sister, Judy. While Judy was sleeping,
Flavia put a tiny doll inside the bassinet and wondered what Judy would
think when she woke up and saw it, and whether or not she would ever
love dolls the way Flavia did.

Willie brought the Christmas Picture Book down from the shelf, and
he and Flavia lay on the floor and began to look at the pages slowly. They
loved looking at pictures of other Christmases, and as they turned the
pages, they talked softly about how it was just like turning pages in Time.
Willie asked, "Why aren't there any pictures of Santa Claus in this
whole book? If there aren't any pictures of him, how do we know what
he really looks like?" he said.

Mama smiled and said, "Close your eyes, Willie, and you can 'picture'
him. Use the magic in your mind...your imagination...and you can see
him. Just 'picture' how you think Santa Claus should look, and what he
really is to you. He may look different to each of us...but if you try real
hard, and believe you can do it...you will see him, I promise. Begin by
remembering that he is someone very special because he gives to others."

The room was quiet for a few minutes, then Daddy began to tell Flavia and Willie where he had been when he wasn't in some of the pictures in the book…and about what he had learned on the Christmases he'd been away.

He told them how, in some other countries, people celebrated different holidays and that not everyone, even in this country, celebrated Christmas. ''There are religions in this country and in others where people believe differently and celebrate with different kinds of food and songs and stories,'' he said, ''and their traditions mean as much to them as Christmas does to us.''

Daddy had been gone a lot, and had lived and worked all over the world. He knew all about holidays and customs and things faraway, and had a special way of talking about the places where he'd been. When he described them, it always made Flavia think she was really there.

She knew that meant she was using her imagination, and she loved it when she could imagine being in some of the places he talked about. He said it was just like going on a magic carpet ride. And to her it was, for that is how Flavia saw the world.

As Flavia looked at the pictures again, she saw how even some of their own Christmases had been different from the rest. It was all pictured there in the book. Some Christmases had tall trees and lots of wrapped presents, and some had little trees and few presents. Sometimes Mama made stars for a manzanita branch, put the branch into a clay pot, and that had been their tree.

There were pictures of Christmases when Flavia and Willie had been babies, and some even before they had been born. Seeing these gave her a funny feeling…because Flavia could never imagine this world without her in it.

But the Christmas she most remembered, was one not pictured in the book… it was the Christmas when Mama had made Flavia a coat from Mama's own coat. There was no money to spend that Christmas and so it was Flavia's only present under the tree. Flavia knew now that the number of presents wasn't important…and that the real gift was knowing that Mama loved her that much.

Whenever she thought of times like this, tears came to her eyes
and a feeling came over her as though the love she felt inside would
overflow…and she knew she would always have these times to
remember, just like those pictures in the book.

She was thinking how much she cared about all the people around her,
and how she wished she could stop time and hold it in her hands…so that
she could keep things just the way they were at that very moment…forever.

It was a feeling she had felt often since Jack had talked to her a long
time ago, when he told her that what she was feeling was a gift…and
that it would be a part of her for as long as she lived.

Every time she felt this way, Flavia wanted to be near Mama.

Mama was still sewing on the doll, so Flavia sat close down beside her. She often would sit there beside Mama while she sewed, and they would talk about things.

Mama knew all about dolls and imaginations, for she was a dollmaker. She made them out of cloth scraps and buttons and yarns and ribbons and lace and threads. But…somehow they all looked like people when she was finished. *Real people.*

Sometimes Flavia would talk to them, dance with them and pretend they were real. Mama made all kinds of dolls…and every year she made angel dolls…but the angel doll Mama was making now was the most beautiful Flavia had ever seen.

In her long angel hair there was a wreath woven of shiny gold ribbons…and her dress was white and filmy and full. Mama had sewn a tiny satin heart on the dress and little gold stars on the hem.

Flavia looked at the angel doll lovingly for a long time before she asked, "Who is it for, Mama? Is it a present?"

"Who it's for is a secret," Mama said, "but it is for someone who will understand what Christmas really means. It is a special doll, a Christmas Angel Doll...and it is filled with love."

While Mama spoke, Flavia saw her glance over at the bassinet and look at little Judy. Then Flavia heard her own thoughts inside, as though they had a voice, and the voice inside was telling her that Mama was making the doll for Judy.

When Flavia looked at the sleeping baby and saw how little she was and how she looked like a baby angel…Flavia understood why Mama would surely give it to her.

And then Flavia heard her thoughts tell her something else…that she would have to remember from now on that Mama would love Judy just as much as she did Willie and her. With that thought, Flavia quickly turned her head so that Mama could not see the tears that filled her eyes.

That night before she fell asleep, Flavia remembered how the
Christmas tree was little again and how Christmas would be even
more different than ever this year because there was a baby sister.

Flavia even wondered if there would be any special gifts for her or
Willie now that they had to share Christmas with someone new. There
had always been one special gift under the tree for each of them and they
were always a little different than the rest.

These were the gifts that were always set aside to be opened later on
Christmas night, after all the rest of the family had gone home.

Then Flavia remembered Willie's questions about Santa Claus, so she closed her eyes and tried to "picture" him. She began to think how Santa Claus should look…and no matter how many times she began to imagine him, the "pictures" in her mind always turned into someone who looked a lot like The Hanky Man, this special man who gathered up broken toys and things, repaired them, then gave them to children.

Except for the red jacket and long white beard that Santa was supposed to have, they looked just the same. There was something else Flavia thought of…how did The Hanky Man always seem to know which toys each child wished for? Maybe he really was Santa Claus. Maybe, when he wasn't in the North Pole, he drove this old red truck down the alley of their street every Tuesday collecting broken toys to fix.

Maybe underneath his red coat, Santa wore an old shirt and red suspenders. And maybe he played a harmonica and sang gypsy songs so full of joy and wonder…that it made Willie and her anxious for Tuesdays to come. She was still thinking about all of the "maybes" when she fell asleep.

It was after breakfast on Christmas Eve morning, and Mama and Mammo sat at the kitchen table working...Mama decorating her bread dough stars for the tree, and Mammo putting icing on the Christmas cookies.

Flavia and Willie listened while Mama told them about when she was a little girl and how her own Papa had taught her about "giving". He had told her that "giving" was a gift itself...and once you understood it, you never forgot what it meant. And that love was the very best gift of all.

Flavia watched Mama's face as she spoke and her hands as they worked. She thought again about how lucky she was to have her. Mama knew more than just about dolls and imaginations...she knew about giving and about love...just like her Papa before her...and Flavia knew that that made Mama strong. Flavia hurried to tell Willie what she was sure of now...both Mama and her Papa before her were angels.

While Flavia and Willie were hanging their stockings alongside Judy's, Willie said, "Flavia, I've been thinking about what Mama said, and how to 'picture' Santa Claus, and I keep 'picturing' him to be just like The Hanky Man. So, I've been wondering...could Santa drive a red truck all year long, and a sleigh with reindeer only at Christmastime? Could his truck become the sleigh...the way Cinderella's pumpkin became a coach?" Willie's eyes widened at the thought of all that wonder.

Flavia didn't tell Willie how her thoughts had been much the same as his the night before. It was Tuesday, and they both knew The Hanky Man would come by today to gather more things to fix and then give away. But Flavia knew they couldn't ask him about all they had been thinking...this was something she'd have to talk to Jack about, because she was sure that all Dream Makers knew about things this wonderful.

But, for now, the questions would go unanswered...and so she busied herself again with the mistletoe and tying it with a ribbon, while Willie put the star on top of the tree and then quietly took a handful of Christmas candy from the tall glass jar on the table.

Suddenly Flavia thought of something, and reached to peek inside the box that had been filled and was waiting for The Hanky Man. She wondered if just *maybe* Mama could be giving the Christmas Angel Doll to The Hanky Man so that he could give it to ''someone who understood what Christmas really meant!''

Although it wasn't in the box, Flavia kept wondering and thinking about the doll. She quietly wished she had asked Mama, even before the Christmas Angel Doll was finished, if she could have held it just once.

That night, after Jack had finished his writing, he waited with Flavia and Willie on the corner 'til the church's big truck picked them up. Willie was very excited as Jack helped him climb into the back of the open truck.

It would be Willie's very first time caroling, and it made him feel very tall. Jack told them both to watch the people's faces as they sang to them.

Willie thought Jack meant they would be surprised, but Flavia remembered something Jack had said to her. "You can see a lot when you look into people's faces," he said, "their feelings and their lives are written there."

With this on her mind, Flavia began to see something different this year. As they sang Christmas songs, she saw a kind of glow come over the people's faces and she realized that by singing for them, they were giving them something magic. This "giving" made her feel good inside, just like Mama had said.

Later that night, she looked out the window and talked to the moon about
all that had happened this day. For a long time now, the moon had been a
kind of special friend to her and before she would go to sleep at night,
she'd often think out loud and tell the moon things she secretly thought
and dreamed of...and about all the wonder she thought was in the world.

The moon and Jack had always listened, no matter what, and now she was unafraid to tell or ask them anything. Sometimes she wondered if Willie also talked to the moon at night. She knew sometimes he talked to one of the cloth rabbits Mama had made. She had heard him.

CHRISTMAS, IT WAS HERE!

Flavia could not remember when they had not had a "crumble-up" breakfast on Christmas morning...and this year she was glad it was the same. "Crumble-up" meant the crumbling of bacon over biscuits and milk gravy.

There were also scrambled eggs and "chow-chow", the sauce Daddy made with tomatoes and onions and chili peppers.

Flavia didn't like the "chow-chow" much...but her favorite was Mama's hot biscuits spread with the apricot jam Mammo made.

The opening of gifts came after breakfast and then in the early afternoon the aunts and uncles and cousins came over, along with some of their neighbors, like Mrs. Spurgeon, who otherwise would have been alone on Christmas.

They all spent the day talking and laughing and taking pictures and singing and telling stories and just being together.

Then it was time to move furniture and arrange things so that there would be room enough for everyone to sit together at one table for Christmas dinner. This was very important to Mama.

Flavia and Willie helped Jack as they shoved three different tables together and covered them with tablecloths so that it would look like one long table.

Flavia knew it really wasn't...and she wished the chairs were all
alike, the way they always were in the pictures in magazines, but those
thoughts quickly left her mind when she saw how wonderful Mama had
made the table look.

She had covered oranges with cloves and wrapped them all in ribbons,
and put one at every plate. It made the whole room smell even more
like Christmas.

The dinner of turkey, cornbread dressing, yams, a salad made of apples and walnuts, and everything else Flavia looked forward to every year was on that long table.

After the pumpkin pie and Christmas cookies, the day had turned into night and the rest of the family and the neighbors began to leave.

Flavia wondered why it always took Christmas such a long time to get here...and then it was over so soon.

But inside she knew it wasn't really over...not yet. In fact, the time she most waited for was now...when everyone else had left and it was just them...the time for Flavia and Willie's special gifts to be opened...the ones that had been set aside for Christmas night.

And this year there had been one more added...the one for baby Judy.

Willie opened his present first. It was a snow globe with angels and stars and all sparkly and wonderful. After Willie turned it upside down and shook it, the snow began to fall over the angels' wings and shine like magic.

When Flavia looked at it, she imagined she was one of those angels and was dancing on a cloud up by the moon, and that the stars were dancing around her like snowflakes. It was a wonderful feeling.

Then Flavia made her quiet wish...and began to open her gift.
And there it was, wrapped in tissue, the present she had secretly
dreamed and hoped for...the Christmas Angel Doll Mama had made.

SHE was the one Mama had been thinking of, the "someone who
would understand what Christmas really means."

She held it close to her heart, looked up at Mama's beautiful face,
and she was so full of love she could not speak.

The last gift was for baby Judy. Hers was small, wrapped in an envelope tied with a golden ribbon.

Jack reached for it under the tree, untied the ribbon and slipped the page out of the envelope.

It was the poem he had been writing on Christmas Eve. He had titled it "Judy's First Christmas" and he began to read...

Judy's First Christmas

The lights are dim
but atop the tree a
star is shining bright.

For in spite
of closing darkness
it's Christmas Eve tonight.

And small hands clasp
at a doll's soft curl
and small eyes open wide.

And a small heart thrills
with happiness
at the presents side by side.

But dear sweet girl,
the things you have
are more than those you see.

The real gifts
at this Christmastime
are not placed on the tree.

a family close
in love and joy,
the care that they can give

the promise
you shall always have,
this country in which to live.

Yes, each may have
his presents
but yours
are more precious, dear,

for you give love
and hope anew
and you give it
by just being here.

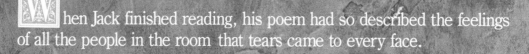

When Jack finished reading, his poem had so described the feelings of all the people in the room that tears came to every face.

Then there was a long silence while the lights on the tree made Mama's bread dough stars suddenly twinkle.

More magic, Flavia thought.

As she put her head to her pillow that night, Flavia could hear Mama rocking Judy to sleep.

But Mama was singing something new tonight, for she had given a tune to the poem Jack had written and was singing it like a song.

Flavia knew what Mama had meant now...that giving love was the real spirit of Christmas.

She also knew that the Christmas Angel Doll which she held onto so tightly now, she would one day give to her own daughter.

And she understood that "giving," like love, is a gift...and the only way to keep love forever is to give it away.

Flavia gave a last look up into the night and saw the Christmas sky and the magic of the moon and stars above her. She heard the faint sound of sleigh bells and began to wonder whether it was coming from the front door or from somewhere in the night sky.

She then smiled and realized it really didn't matter from where the sound was coming, it only mattered that she had heard it.

As she closed her eyes she thought of all the love and wonder that had been given that Christmas and she hoped she would never forget this night.

Flavia didn't know that by this time, having finished rocking the baby, Mama was now standing at the half opened door and heard her as she said her prayers.

And she didn't see Mama smile or the tear of love that rolled down her cheek when she heard Flavia softly whisper, just before she fell asleep . . .

... "Merry Christmas world...I love you."

the end...

EPILOGUE

Flavia would always remember that very special Christmas...and years later she and Willie and Judy would each sing the song Mama had sung, the one from Jack's poem. They would sing it to their own children while rocking them to sleep.

Flavia would still make bread dough stars for the manzanita tree and would give an angel doll to her daughter every Christmas. And sometimes, at night, Flavia would still talk to the moon.

On that Christmas night so long ago, Flavia could not have known that her life would be a gift woven of hopes and dreams...and that it would always be filled with love and surprises.

But most of all, Flavia could not have known so long ago that love is more than a gift...it is a most precious legacy. A legacy we give our children...so that they will have it to give to their children.

Love does indeed live forever...for it is a part of the wonder and the magic that is spilled upon this earth.

Merry Christmas, dear world.

RECIPE FOR BREAD DOUGH STARS

INGREDIENTS:

4 Cups Flour
1 Cup Salt
1 Cup Water

1. Preheat oven to 350 degrees.
2. Mix ingredients together with your hands. If mixture is too dry or stiff, slowly add a little more water.
3. After thoroughly mixing, knead dough for 4 to 5 minutes.
4. Using a rolling pin, roll dough out like pie crust.
5. Use star-shaped cookie cutter to form stars in dough. (For less perfectly shaped stars, use an ordinary table knife and draw stars into the dough).
6. Near top of each star, with a pencil, make a hole large enough so that a gold thread or cord (or fishing line) can be strung through it to become a hanger.
7. Bake for approximately one hour. Make sure to check for doneness with toothpick. You'll know the stars are ready when the dough is no longer soft.
8. After stars have cooled on wax paper, apply glue that dries clear and sprinkle with glitter.
9. Tie ribbon, gold thread or fishing line through the hole in each star and hang on tree.

Please note: Bread Dough Stars are for decorative purposes only and are not meant to be eaten.